Prayers
FROM
Grandma

"Hannah Grace Mettler
TO

Margaret Mary Mettler
FROM

7/26/08
DATE   For   10th B'day

PRAYERS FROM GRANDMA

Copyright © 1998 Becky L. Amble

Published by Garborg's, Inc.
P.O. Box 20132
Bloomington, MN 55420

Design by Jennifer Parker

ISBN 1-58375-421-0

ACKNOWLEDGMENTS

All The Grandmothers

Thank you to all of the people who passed out my questionnaires, and especially to all of the women who took the time to write their prayers, verses, and poems. I wish we could have used everyone's material.

All of the grandmothers have given me permission to use their first name, initial of their last name, year of birth, and either home town or current residence.

Becky L. Amble is an accomplished businesswoman, marketer, and researcher. She has been cited as a trend-spotter by The Wall Street Journal and USA Today. She works at the Minneapolis StarTribune as a group leader and marketing manager in the rentals market group. She is also involved with several professional, civic, and community groups.

Becky grew up in North Dakota and now lives with her husband, Marshall Gravdahl, their son, Alex, and two cats, AlleyCat and Greta, in Woodbury, Minnesota.

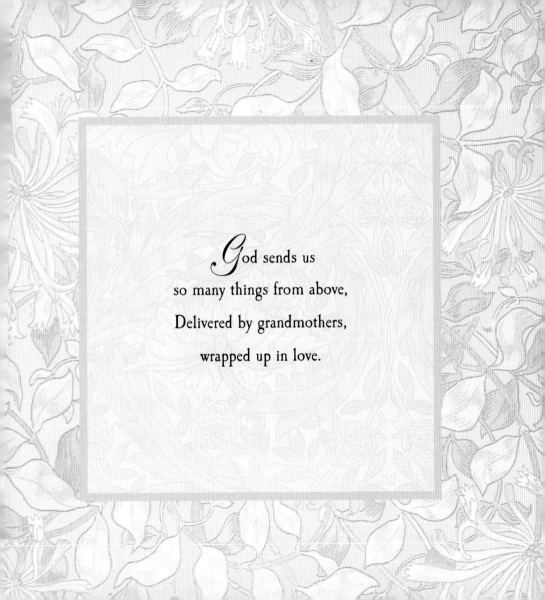

God sends us
so many things from above,
Delivered by grandmothers,
wrapped up in love.

We thank You, Lord, for the grandchildren all over the world that have brought so much joy to so many people. We thank You for our own grandchildren that have been such a blessing to us. Help us to be examples for them; teach, guide, and encourage them to live their lives according to Your will. Watch over them with Your loving care and keep them safe from harm. Amen.

KATHLEEN O., 1921; TWO RIVERS, WIS.

TO LIVE IN PRAYER TOGETHER
IS TO WALK IN LOVE TOGETHER.

MARGARET MOORE JACOBS

WE CLOSE OUR EYES

We close our eyes, we bow our heads
and offer thanks for daily bread.
For friends and family gathered near
for forests and rivers for elk and deer.
For oceans and mountains for plant and stone
for all that we feel for love, beauty and home.
And our children shall sit with their own children small,
and give thanks, once again, for the miracle of it all.

STEVE MYRVANG

*H*e will keep in perfect peace all those who trust in him,
whose thoughts turn often to the Lord!

ISAIAH 26:3 TLB

*L*ord, our only source of perfect peace, help us to find
strength in silence as we recognize Your voice and find our
way to You amidst the earthly chaos of our daily lives. Thank You
for hearing our prayers. Help us listen for Your direction. Amen.

DOROTHY G., 1942; WYOMING, MINN.

*H*eavenly Father, today is my grandson's first baseball game. He's been waiting a long time for this day. We're so proud of him, just as we were so proud of his father when he played Little League baseball. Help him to learn how important it is to be a good sport. Help him to know how to win as well as how to lose. May he always remember that making a home run or catching a fly ball is not as important as keeping his mind and body clean and fit, so that he can always do his best at whatever he attempts. May baseball help to make him a winner in the game of life. Amen.

THEDA W., 1924; COLD SPRING, KY.

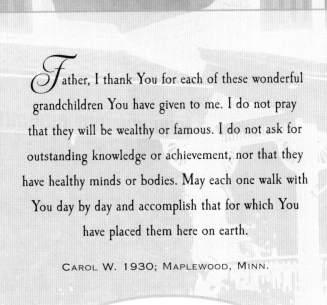

Father, I thank You for each of these wonderful grandchildren You have given to me. I do not pray that they will be wealthy or famous. I do not ask for outstanding knowledge or achievement, nor that they have healthy minds or bodies. May each one walk with You day by day and accomplish that for which You have placed them here on earth.

CAROL W. 1930; MAPLEWOOD, MINN.

PRAYER CHANGES THINGS.
TRUST IN THE LORD.

RUTH R.; FORT DODGE, IOWA

YOU DO NOT WALK ALONE

BY MARY MARGARET WITTNER

*Y*ou do not walk a lonely road for God is always near.
He shares your heartbreak and your pain and knows the things
you fear. His hand will guide you safely for His love is always
there, to give you strength and courage, if you ask for it in prayer.

ALBERTA R., 1928; FINLAYSAN, MINN.

*G*od cares what happens...even more than you do. He pays
even greater attention to you, down to the last detail—even
numbering the hairs on your head!

MATTHEW 10:30-31 MSG

The Lord's Prayer

*O*ur Father who art in heaven,

Hallowed be thy name.

Thy kingdom come.

Thy will be done, on earth as it is in heaven.

Give us this day our daily bread.

And forgive us our debts;

as we forgive our debtors.

And lead us not into temptation;

but deliver us from evil.

For Thine is the kingdom,

the power, and the glory,

forever and ever. Amen.

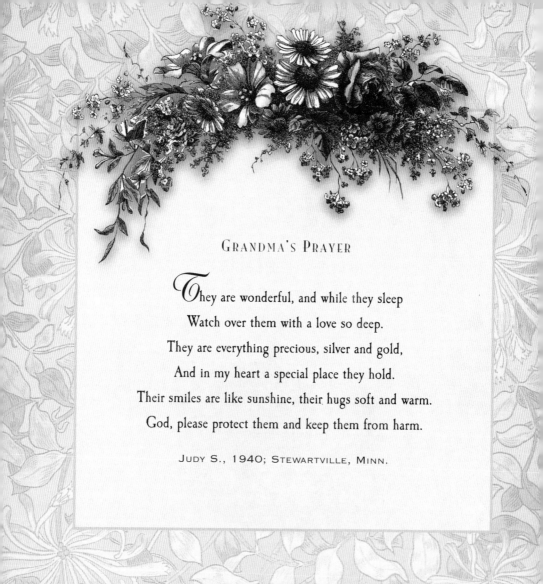

GRANDMA'S PRAYER

They are wonderful, and while they sleep
Watch over them with a love so deep.
They are everything precious, silver and gold,
And in my heart a special place they hold.
Their smiles are like sunshine, their hugs soft and warm.
God, please protect them and keep them from harm.

JUDY S., 1940; STEWARTVILLE, MINN.

Oh, Bless Their Heart!

*M*y father's mother, who was born in 1895 in Omaha, used to say this about anyone she heard me mention. It didn't matter if it was a male or female, someone in trouble, or someone doing well. I now realize she was really blessing them. What a loving response, and a memorable one, as well.

Sally K., 1938; Omaha, Neb.

This is the day the Lord has made; we will rejoice and be glad in it.

Psalm 118:24 NKJV

GRANDMA

*M*y grandma likes to play with God,
They have a kind of game.
She plants the garden full of seeds,
He sends the sun and rain.
She likes to sit and talk with God
And knows He is right there.
She prays about the whole wide world,
Then leaves us in His care.

ANN JOHNSON, AGE 8

$\mathcal{D}$ear Lord Jesus, please watch over my grandchildren and guide them. Holy Spirit, live within them and give them Your peace. Give them strength to say "no" to drugs and alcohol. Help them to have a personal relationship with You. May they learn to love and be loved. In Jesus' name I pray. Amen.

JANELL F., 1935; WOODBURY, MINN.

$\mathcal{I}$n everything you do, put God first, and he will direct you and crown your efforts with success.

PROVERBS 3:6 TLB

*M*y maternal grandmother was a woman of great spiritual
strength and love.... When I was a small child, she taught me to pray.
I spent many nights with her, and our bedtime ritual always began
with a prayer and blessings for the family.

Today, my 91-year-old paternal grandmother is a living inspiration,
and I am awed by her positive thinking and energy. She believes
every day is a gift and she is thankful for every experience. Her great
positive spirit is a shining example to those of us who will keep her
legacy. I have been truly blessed with two loving, spiritual grandmothers.
I pray that I may carry on their legacy for generations to come.

LAUREN S., 1950; TACOMA, WASH.

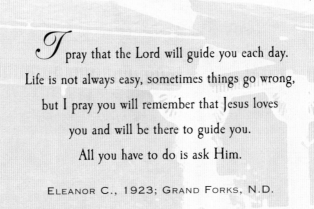

$\mathcal{I}$ pray that the Lord will guide you each day.
Life is not always easy, sometimes things go wrong,
but I pray you will remember that Jesus loves
you and will be there to guide you.
All you have to do is ask Him.

ELEANOR C., 1923; GRAND FORKS, N.D.

TRAIN UP A CHILD IN
THE WAY HE SHOULD GO: AND
WHEN HE IS OLD, HE WILL NOT
DEPART FROM IT.

PROVERBS 22:6 KJV

$\mathcal{T}$ake time to be quiet and talk to God. Enjoy the beauty of creation and preserve it. Above all, give God the glory in all good things that come your way.

MAE LOU T., 1934; BERESFORD, S.D.

PRAYER

Prayer is so simple

It is like quietly opening a door

And slipping into the very presence of God,

There in the stillness to listen for His voice.

Perhaps to petition or only to listen,

It matters not; just to be there,

In His presence, is prayer!

Father we thank Thee for the night
And for the pleasant morning light
For rest and food and loving care
And all that makes the day so fair.
Help us to do the things we should
To be to others kind and good
In all we do, in all we say,
to grow more loving every day. Amen.

(by Rebecca J. Weston)

DOROTHY F., 1924; EDEN PRAIRIE, MINN.

*H*e prayeth best who loveth best
All things both great and small;
For the dear God who loveth us,
He made and loveth all.

(by Samuel Taylor Coleridge)

MARJORIE G., 1937; THOMPSON, N.D.

A CHILD'S PRAYER
BY ALBERT SCHWEITZER

O heavenly Father, protect and bless all things that have breath:
guard them from all evil and let them sleep in peace.

*C*reator and Father of us all, Thank You for the joy of being a grandmother, for the beautiful, ambitious, committed children and grandchildren with which You have blessed me. Keep them safe and healthy and focused in the everyday routine of their lives. Wrap Your loving arms around them. Bring wholeness and peace to their hearts. Amen.

ROSALIE S.; FRANKFORT, KY.

THANKS

ear Lord, we give Thee thanks

for the bright silent moon

And thanks for the sun

that will warm us at noon.

And thanks for the stars

and the quick running breeze,

And thanks for the shade

and the straightness of trees.

WE THANK THEE
FOR HEALTH AND FOOD,
FOR LOVE AND FRIENDS, FOR
EVERYTHING THY GOODNESS SENDS.

RALPH WALDO EMERSON

*O*ne hundred years from now it will not matter what kind of car

you drove, what kind of house you lived in, how much you had in your

bank account, or what your clothes looked like. But the world may be

a little better because you were important in the life of a child.

(by Margaret Fishback Powers)

JEAN H., 1919; BAGLEY, MINN.

*M*ore things are wrought by prayer than this world dreams of.

(by Alfred, Lord Tennyson)

MONA R., 1932; SHAKOPEE, MINN.

PROTECTION

Angels circling round my head,

Angels watching by my bed,

Angels keeping me from harm,

Angels cradling me in their arms,

Every day and every night,

In darkest dark, or lightest light.

Sent from God to protect from above,

Sent from God to show me love.

It is a wonderful thing to see

Just how safe with them I'll be.

JUDY S., 1940;
STEWARTVILLE, MINN.

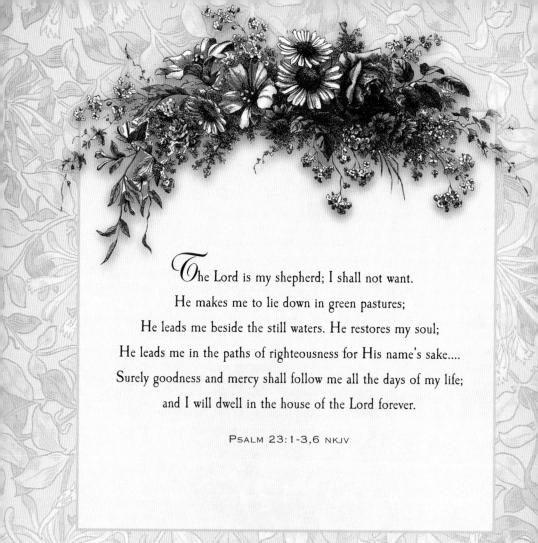

The Lord is my shepherd; I shall not want.

He makes me to lie down in green pastures;

He leads me beside the still waters. He restores my soul;

He leads me in the paths of righteousness for His name's sake....

Surely goodness and mercy shall follow me all the days of my life;

and I will dwell in the house of the Lord forever.

PSALM 23:1-3,6 NKJV

I am holding in my arms the most beautiful gift I have ever received, wrapped in a pink blanket—a brand new granddaughter. I pray that Your plan for her life will ultimately be fulfilled. May she never doubt Your unconditional love. May she be willing to let You mold her and make her after Your will. Help me to be a grandma that she can always count on to listen, but not judge; to accept, but not condemn; to love, but not preach; to make precious memories which she will always treasure. Oh Lord, make me always worthy of this precious gift. Amen.

THEDA W., 1924; COLD SPRING, KY.

FATHER, FOR YOUR UNENDING CARE AND MANY BLESSINGS I DEEPLY THANK YOU. MAY THAT BRING PEACE AND REST AT THE END OF THE DAY.

ESTHER S., 1904; ST. PAUL, MINN.

$\mathcal{D}$ear God, thank You for this day. May we rejoice and be glad in it. Be with me and guide me in the things I have to do. Be with my children and grandchildren. Give them a happy, safe, and caring home. Give them faith that continues to grow stronger. Help them to be patient, kind, and understanding. Continually remind them of your many blessings. In Jesus' name, Amen.

IRENE S., 1938; GRAND FORKS, N.D.

TABLE PRAYER

*G*od is great. God is good.
Let us thank Him for this food.
By His hand we all are fed.
Give us, Lord, our daily bread. Amen.

IRENE S., 1938; GRAND FORKS, N.D.

*B*e joyful always; pray continuously; give thanks
in all circumstances, for this is God's will for you.

I THESSALONIANS 5:16-18 NIV

Below is our Norwegian Table prayer, passed down for at least five generations. We still say it together as a family (17 of us) on special days and holidays. Even the youngest grandchildren know it.

I Jesu nave gar vi til bords
At spise og drikke pa ditt ord
Dig Gud til aere, oss til gavn
a far vi mat i Jesu navn.

In Jesus' name we come to the table
To eat and drink on Your Word
Thou God, to honor, for us a gain
So we eat our food in Jesus' name.

IRENE F., 1923; ANOKA, MINN.

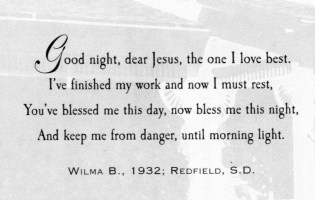

$\mathcal{G}$ood night, dear Jesus, the one I love best.

I've finished my work and now I must rest,

You've blessed me this day, now bless me this night,

And keep me from danger, until morning light.

WILMA B., 1932; REDFIELD, S.D.

GIVE ME TIME TO TELL
THIS NEW GENERATION (AND
THEIR CHILDREN TOO) ABOUT ALL
YOUR MIGHTY MIRACLES.

PSALM 71:18 TLB

There is no more significant involvement in another's life than prevailing, consistent prayer. It is more helpful than a gift of money, more encouraging than a strong sermon, more effective than a compliment, more reassuring than a physical embrace.

CHARLES R. SWINDOLL

The Lord is my light and my salvation; Whom shall I fear? The Lord is the strength of my life; Of whom shall I be afraid?

PSALM 27:1 NKJV

Guard Me

ear Father in heaven,

Look down from above.

Bless papa and mama,

And those whom I love.

May angels guard over

My slumber, and when

The morning is breaking

Awake me. Amen.

Blanche G., 1910;
Minneapolis, Minn.

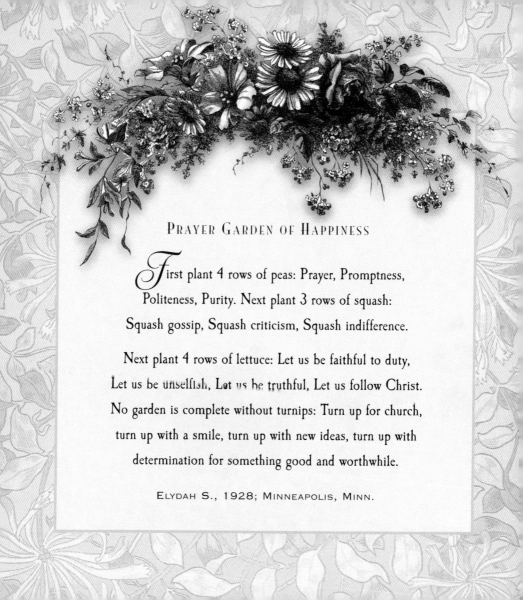

Prayer Garden of Happiness

First plant 4 rows of peas: Prayer, Promptness,
Politeness, Purity. Next plant 3 rows of squash:
Squash gossip, Squash criticism, Squash indifference.

Next plant 4 rows of lettuce: Let us be faithful to duty,
Let us be unselfish, Let us be truthful, Let us follow Christ.
No garden is complete without turnips: Turn up for church,
turn up with a smile, turn up with new ideas, turn up with
determination for something good and worthwhile.

Elydah S., 1928; Minneapolis, Minn.

$\mathcal{T}$hank You, Jesus, for this day,

For my food, and for my play.

Now my evening thanks I bring

For my home and everything.

Bless me as I sleep this night,

Wake me with the morning light.

MARIE C. TURK

BLESSED IS THE MAN WHO TRUSTS
IN THE LORD AND HAS MADE THE
LORD HIS HOPE AND CONFIDENCE.

JEREMIAH 17:7 TLB

*M*y prayer for you, my grandchild, is the same
one I said over your mommy and your auntie every
night until they left home to marry:
Now to Him who is able to keep you from stumbling
and to present you faultless before the presence of His
glory with exceeding joy, to God our Savior, who alone
is wise, be glory and majesty, dominion and power,
both now and forever. Amen. (Jude 1:24-25)

BEVERLY C., 1939; BLOOMINGTON, MINN.

$\mathcal{D}$on't worry about anything; instead, pray about everything;

tell God your needs and don't forget to thank him for his

answers. If you do this you will experience God's peace, which is

far more wonderful than the human mind can understand.

PHILIPPIANS 4:6-7 TLB

$\mathcal{A}$ grandmother has ears that truly listen;

arms that always hold.

She has a love that's never-ending,

and a heart made of purest gold.

Gracious Father, God of love and compassion, into Your
care, I place my many grandchildren. I believe that You
will watch over them. I am growing old and cannot always
be there for them. Utmost in my heart is a prayer that all
my grandchildren and great-grandchildren remain close
and faithful to You. Having You, a greater One, to
watch over them gives me peace and joy.

NORA S., 1913; WATERTOWN, S.D.

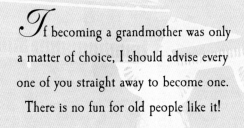

If becoming a grandmother was only
a matter of choice, I should advise every
one of you straight away to become one.
There is no fun for old people like it!

HANNAH WHITALL SMITH

I ALONE KNOW MY
PURPOSE FOR YOU, SAYS THE LORD:
PROSPERITY AND NOT MISFORTUNE, AND
A LONG LINE OF CHILDREN AFTER YOU.

JEREMIAH 29:11 NEB

PRAYER OF THANKSGIVING

*D*ear God, thank You for watching over our children and grandchildren, protecting and guiding them, providing for all their needs of body and soul. Also for watching over my husband, myself, and all our family and friends. For all of these things I give you my heartfelt thanks. Amen.

MONA R., 1932; SHAKOPEE, MINN.

*W*hatever you ask for in prayer, believe that you have received it, and it will be yours.

MARK 11:24 NIV

Our Father in Heaven,
Thank You that we may
call You our Father, that we are Your
children. Lord, I pray that each one of our
children, our grandchildren, and great-grandchildren
may know You as their personal Savior. May we
meet in Heaven and spend eternity with You.
In Jesus' name. Amen.

RUTH S., 1909; ADAMS, N.D.

$\mathcal{D}$ear Jesus, You know how much every boy
wants a puppy. But my little grandson can't have one
because of allergies. Today he's going to get a pet snake.
His mother and sister have both said they won't touch it—ever.
He has asked me if I'll hold it. Lord, you know I'm afraid.
Even thinking about it frightens me. Will You give me the
courage to hold the snake so I can show him that what
means a lot to him, means just as much to me?
I thank You, Father, that You have made
all creatures, great and small. Amen.

THEDA W., 1924; COLD SPRING, KY.

You were created by Me, I gave life to you,

You are the image of Me, I abide in you.

You are the work of My hand, I am pleased with you.

You are a part of My plan, I believe in you.

MARY ANN B., 1919; WELLS, MINN.

THE LORD WATCH BETWEEN
ME AND THEE, WHEN WE ARE
ABSENT ONE FROM ANOTHER.

GENESIS 31:49 KJV

WEDDING PRAYER

*D*ear Heavenly Father, today is my daughter's wedding day.
They have chosen to speak their vows under the blue skies with
You watching down from the heavens with family and friends nearby.
Dear Lord, give them a marriage filled with happiness and love
as strong and lasting as the mountains themselves.
We know there will be times in their lives filled with sunshine
and times filled with rain. But as You kiss the flowers on the
hillside with sunshine and send them rain to strengthen and grow,
help their love to strengthen and grow for each other. Heavenly Father,
bless them with joy and keep them safe in Your love.
P.S. Dear Lord, I would also love more grandchildren! Amen.

DOROTHY C., 1943; BRICELYN, MINN.

Thank You, Lord, for the special blessing of grandchildren. Please send guardian angels to watch over them and keep them from harm. Guide them in thought, word, and deed that they may live their lives according to Your plan.

BETTY A., 1934; BLUE EARTH, MINN.

May my grandchildren "seek first the kingdom of God and His righteousness," and may "all these things be added unto [them]."

(Taken from Matthew 6:33 NKJV)

JEAN V., 1930; JACKSONVILLE, FLA.

*D*ear Lord, of all the blessings You have bestowed upon me, one of the most precious is being a grandmother. There is such joy in watching these children of my children. Everything is a new and wonderful adventure for them as they grow and mature. They help me see things in a new and better way. They put things in their proper perspective. They share their secrets and their dreams, and in their sharing, I see the face of Christ. I thank You for the togetherness we share in this life, and I pray that we can spend eternity together. Amen.

SYLVIA W., 1938; SYRACUSE, N.Y.

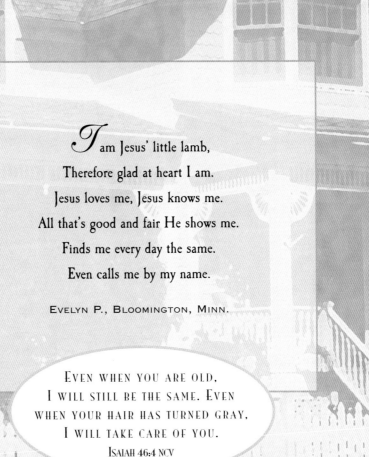

I am Jesus' little lamb,
Therefore glad at heart I am.
Jesus loves me, Jesus knows me.
All that's good and fair He shows me.
Finds me every day the same.
Even calls me by my name.

EVELYN P., BLOOMINGTON, MINN.

EVEN WHEN YOU ARE OLD,
I WILL STILL BE THE SAME. EVEN
WHEN YOUR HAIR HAS TURNED GRAY,
I WILL TAKE CARE OF YOU.
ISAIAH 46:4 NCV

$\mathcal{G}$od keeps his promise, and he will not allow you to be tested beyond your power to remain firm; at the time you are put to the test, he will give you the strength to endure it and so provide you with a way out. (1 Corinthians 10:13 paraphrased)

MARGARET M., 1942; WARNERS, N.Y.

$\mathcal{Y}$our life is the answer to someone's prayers.

$\mathcal{G}$ood and gracious God,

Remember my grandchildren

And shower them with Your love and mercy.

Notice the good and delightful things about them.

Do away with or reform all that displeases You.

Make of them that which You desire.

Offer them Your guidance and care.

Thank You for Your gift of life.

How grateful I am for these,

the children of my children.

LYN L., 1939;
ARDEN HILLS, MINN.

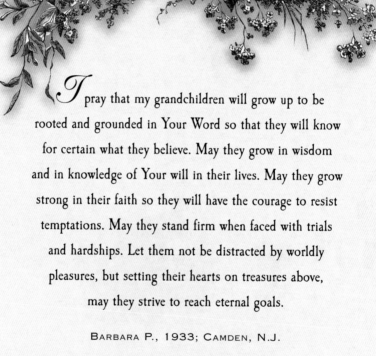

$\mathcal{I}$ pray that my grandchildren will grow up to be rooted and grounded in Your Word so that they will know for certain what they believe. May they grow in wisdom and in knowledge of Your will in their lives. May they grow strong in their faith so they will have the courage to resist temptations. May they stand firm when faced with trials and hardships. Let them not be distracted by worldly pleasures, but setting their hearts on treasures above, may they strive to reach eternal goals.

BARBARA P., 1933; CAMDEN, N.J.

What God Hath Promised
by Annie Johnson Flint

*G*od hath not promised skies always blue,

Flower-strewn pathways all our lives through,

God hath not promised sun without rain,

Joy without sorrow, peace without pain,

But God hath promised strength for the day,

Rest for the labor, light for the way;

Grace for the trials, help from above,

Unfailing sympathy, undying love.

Jackie O., 1944; Dawson, Minn.

Come, Lord Jesus, be our guest,
and let these gifts to us be
blessed. Amen.

Eleanor S., 1911; Storden, Minn.

$\mathcal{D}$ear Heavenly Father, bless each of our children and grandchildren this day. Keep them safe in the bosom of Your love. May the Holy Spirit always be present to lead and guide them. Especially be with each grandchild so they make the right life choices and choose the correct path to follow.

Thank You for giving them to us to love and enjoy.

In Your name, I pray. Amen.

EVELYN L., 1926; WELCOME, MINN.

*G*reat God, the giver of all good,
Accept our thanks and bless our food,
Grace, health, and strength to us afford.
Through Jesus Christ, our risen Lord. Amen.

KATHLEEN O., 1921; TWO RIVERS, WIS.

A PRAYER FOR GRANDCHILDREN

*D*ear Jesus, as a hen covers her chicks with her wings
to keep them safe...this night protect my grandchildren
under Your golden wings. Amen.

JANET W., 1936; THOMPSON, N.D.

Creator, You have blessed me so many times in my life with Your love and constant support, with a healthy body in which to journey...and with the glorious gift of three wonderful children. But Your goodness never ends, and now You bless me with the great joy of grandchildren—the dessert of life. I pray that they will know and honor both You and themselves. I pray that they will be filled with wonder for the mysteries of life, and I pray that they will always be grateful for the unending blessings which You bestow. I love you, Creator. Thank You, thank You, thank You.

JULIE T., 1952; BLOOMINGTON, MINN.

$\mathcal{D}$ear Heavenly Father, I thank You for all You are to me, and for the many answered prayers throughout my life. I thank You for my children and grandchildren and pray Your continued guidance for them. When we are summoned from here, may we each have Eternal Life with You in heaven through faith in Jesus. May we each live according to Your will.

FREDA G., 1916; MINNETONKA, MINN.

CHILDREN'S CHILDREN ARE A CROWN TO THE AGED, AND PARENTS ARE THE PRIDE OF THEIR CHILDREN.

PROVERBS 17:6 NIV

*G*racious God, who in perfect Love created us as children in Your image, bless the children and grandchildren You have given us with renewed faith and openness to Your living presence. May their footsteps this day follow the way of love taught by Jesus, that His joy may be perfected in them. In Jesus' name, Amen.

MARJORIE C., 1921; GREENFIELD, IOWA

*G*od is our refuge and strength, an ever-present help in trouble.

PSALM 46:1 NIV

I said a prayer for you today
and I know God must have heard,
I felt the answer in my heart although He spoke
no word. I asked that He'd be near you
at the start of each new day, to grant you health
and blessings and friends to share the way.
I asked for happiness for you in all things great
and small, but it was His loving care
I prayed for most of all.

*F*or Grandson: My dear heavenly Father, today I am filled
with joy and praise. I am holding in my arms our first grandchild.
It awes me to see the perfection which You have bestowed upon him.
I pray that You will give him a special measure of Your love.
Watch over him, protect him, care for him, and bless him as he
grows from childhood to manhood. May he become the person
You would have him to be. May his life be filled with thoughtfulness,
kindness, love, joy, and peace. I pray that those who know
him will say of him: "He walks with God."

EVELYN G., 1936; RED LAKE FALLS, MINN.

The God who made your children will hear
your petitions. He has promised to do so.
After all, He loves them more than you do.

DR. JAMES DOBSON

Beloved, I pray that you may prosper in all things and be
in health, just as your soul prospers.... I have no greater joy
than to hear that my children walk in truth.

3 JOHN 1:2,4 NKJV

PLEDGE

Yesterday is beyond reach—its influence is only as great as I permit it to be. I shall not allow it to dim Today—from which I shall accept all the love, joy, fulfillment, and perfection it may offer, confident that as Tomorrow becomes today it also will bear many good things for my appreciation and enrichment if I will only accept them.

WRIGHT S., 1909; NORTHFIELD, MINN.

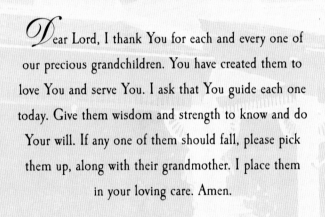

Dear Lord, I thank You for each and every one of our precious grandchildren. You have created them to love You and serve You. I ask that You guide each one today. Give them wisdom and strength to know and do Your will. If any one of them should fall, please pick them up, along with their grandmother. I place them in your loving care. Amen.

ELIZABETH S., 1931; HALLOCK, MINN.

WITH GREAT SWEETNESS,
WITH NATURAL SIMPLICITY...OFFER
YOUR PRAISE TO GOD WITH THE WHOLE
OF YOUR HEART AND SOUL.

MOTHER TERESA

I pray that my family will walk in such a way
that we may look forward to being a family in heaven,
God's family. Not because of what we do or don't do,
but by accepting what God, in Christ, has done.

BESSIE E., 1906; SISSETON, S.D.

*T*rust in the Lord with all your heart,
And lean not on your own understanding;
In all your ways acknowledge Him,
And He shall direct your paths.

PROVERBS 3:5-6 NKJV

AN OLD ENGLISH PRAYER

Give us, Lord, a bit o' sun,
A bit o' work and a bit o' fun...
Give us health our keep to make
And a bit to spare for others' sake.

Give us, too, a bit o' song,
And a tale and a book to help us along.

Give us, Lord, a chance to be
Our goodly best, brave, wise, and free,
Our goodly best for ourselves and others
Till all men learn to live as brothers.

IRENE F., 1923; ANOKA, MINN.

*L*oving God, I am sitting here holding my little granddaughter and by my side stands her brother. How special it is to welcome another grandchild. An adorable little girl who will be the joy of our lives. How can I adequately say thank you? Guide her little feet through the pathway of life. Keep her physically safe and emotionally safe, as well. Help her withstand the temptations that will come. Make her strong and healthy. I especially ask You to give the parents of our precious grandchildren wisdom and understanding as they are with them day by day, guiding and teaching them as they grow. Fill their home with love and joy to give them the secure environment they need. Help us to be the kind of grandparents we should be, ever supportive, loving, and caring. Thank You again, dear Lord, for the wonder of grandchildren!

EVELYN G., 1936; RED LAKE FALLS, MINN.

*M*y children, love must not be a matter of words or talk;
it must be genuine, and show itself in action.

1 JOHN 3:18 NEB

*D*ear God, You know all of our wants and needs before
we ask. As a grandmother, my prayers are the same for my
grandchildren as they were for my children. Grant them wisdom
to not be afraid of what life hands them, but to come to
You in prayer so they can handle the problems and
blessings they are given. Thank You!

DARLENE H., 1936; GRAND FORKS, N.D.

A Lullaby Song

*L*ullaby and good night,

Go to bed now and sleep tight.

Close your eyes and start to yawn,

Pleasant dreams until the dawn.

When the sun lights the sky,

you will wake feeling spry.

Start the day with a smile,

Life is really worthwhile.

MARY R., 1946; AKRON, COLO.

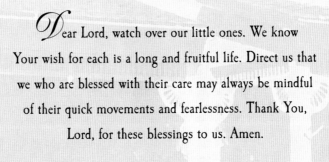

Dear Lord, watch over our little ones. We know Your wish for each is a long and fruitful life. Direct us that we who are blessed with their care may always be mindful of their quick movements and fearlessness. Thank You, Lord, for these blessings to us. Amen.

JOANNE R., 1937; REYNOLDS, N.D.

GIVE THANKS TO THE LORD,
FOR HE IS GOOD;
HIS LOVE ENDURES FOREVER.

PSALM 107:1 NIV

*I*nto my heart, into my heart,

Come into my heart, Lord Jesus.

Come in today, come in to stay,

Come into my heart, Lord Jesus.

MARJORIE G., 1937; THOMPSON, N.D.

*F*or God so loved the world that He gave His

only begotten Son, that whoever believes in Him

should not perish but have everlasting life.

JOHN 3:16 NKJV

$\mathcal{T}$hank You for the

night of rest

and for the morning light;

Watch over us the whole day long

and help us to do right.

All through this day we humbly pray

Be Thou our guard and guide;

Our sins forgive and let us live

close by Thy side. Amen.

MARGARET R., 1922;
TAYLOR'S FALLS, MINN

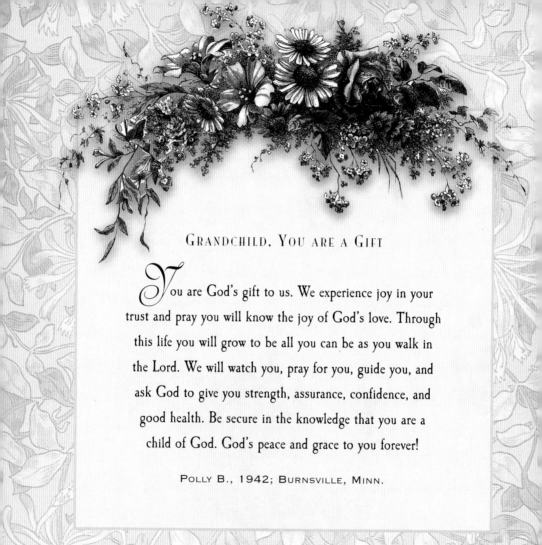

GRANDCHILD, YOU ARE A GIFT

*Y*ou are God's gift to us. We experience joy in your trust and pray you will know the joy of God's love. Through this life you will grow to be all you can be as you walk in the Lord. We will watch you, pray for you, guide you, and ask God to give you strength, assurance, confidence, and good health. Be secure in the knowledge that you are a child of God. God's peace and grace to you forever!

POLLY B., 1942; BURNSVILLE, MINN.

*T*hank You, Lord, for allowing me to be a grandmother; what a wonderful and precious gift grandchildren are. Help me, Lord, to speak Your words and touch their lives in such a way that they may follow You. My heart yearns for all my family to be gathered together in an unbroken circle around You in heaven. This is my prayer.

KATHY W., 1944; MENTOR, MINN.

MY CHILD, DO NOT FORGET MY TEACHING, BUT LET YOUR HEART KEEP MY COMMANDMENTS.

PROVERBS 3:1 NRSV

My Prayer as a Grandma

*D*ear Lord, may I be an influence on my children and grandchildren—to be compassionate, loving, and giving individuals who believe in themselves, can stand up for what is right, and are not fearful of failures. Help them to see failure as a learning experience and obstacles as opportunities to grow. Most of all, help me to instill in them the realization that you are a saving, caring, and consistent God who is there for them when no one else may be. May they be aware of the eternal significance of everything they do, but at the same time, may they not sweat the small things.

MARY R., 1946; AKRON, COLO.

GIVE THANKS

*O*h, give thanks to Him who made

Morning light and evening shade;

Source and giver of all good,

Nightly sleep, and daily food,

Quickener of our wearied powers;

Guard of our unconscious hours.

Jesus, Savior, wash away

all the wrong we've done today.

Help us every day to be

good and gentle, more like Thee. Amen.

KATHY T., 1948; GAYLORD, MINN.

*P*recious Jesus, Creator of all, we give You thanks for our children and grandchildren. Protect them and keep them from all danger. Guide them in their choices, that they will grow to know You and love You as You love them. I ask this in Your Holy name. Amen.

TWYLA J., 1939; REYNOLDS, N.D.

*G*od has not given us the spirit of fear, but of power and of love and of a sound mind.

2 TIMOTHY 1:7 NKJV

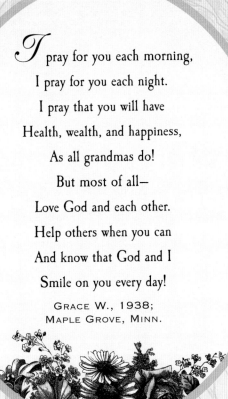

I pray for you each morning,
I pray for you each night.
I pray that you will have
Health, wealth, and happiness,
As all grandmas do!
But most of all—
Love God and each other.
Help others when you can
And know that God and I
Smile on you every day!

GRACE W., 1938;
MAPLE GROVE, MINN.

Dear Lord, we thank You for the privilege of grandparenting. We ask for Your blessings and guidance for all of our dear grandchildren. We know You also love them so, and we ask You to hold them in the palm of Your hand. May they always look to You for guidance. Amen.

KATHY R., 1928; SHOREVIEW, MINN.

$\mathcal{I}$ pray that my children and all my grandchildren would have Jesus in their hearts...that they would know and feel our Father's love and be guided by the Holy Spirit in their daily lives...that they would understand that our Christian faith is our richest treasure.

CHERYL K., 1948; NORTHWOOD, N.D.

DON'T BE ANXIOUS ABOUT TOMORROW. GOD WILL TAKE CARE OF YOUR TOMORROW TOO. LIVE ONE DAY AT A TIME.

MATTHEW 6:34 TLB

I pray that each day you live, you will be grateful you are alive another day. Do what you can for others to help them along the way. We can't always have sunshine as we go down life's path. We also need life's storm clouds to bring the rainbow's glow. With faith and trust we'll conquer each challenge that we meet. So, at the end of the day be content with who you are and be happy. My happiness lies in knowing that when my day is done, I have helped someone find their place in the sun.

You have my love and prayers always.

ZONA M., 1907; SAN LEANDRO, CALIF.

PRAYER OF PROTECTION

The light of God surrounds me;
The love of God enfolds me;
The power of God protects me;
The presence of God watches over me.
Wherever I am, God is.

GRANDCHILD

God, You love children; all girls and boys.

Reach into their hearts with peace and great joys.

And when they're in school or with their peers,

Nestle them under Your wings, through the years.

Divinely lead them through every day.

Capture their hearts in Your own tender way.

Hold their souls safely for eternal life.

In all their future, help calm any strife.

Lead them to Jesus, that they may live,

Doing His will, as their hearts they give.

SHEILA C., 1930; MARSHFIELD, WIS.